We Are Not Enemies After All

Restoring Civility in an Age of Division

Rickhail Campbell

Copyright © 2025 Rickhail Campbell

All rights reserved. This book or any portion thereof may not be reproduced or used in any manner whatsoever without the express written permission of the publisher, except for the use of brief quotations in a book review.

Printed in the United States of America

First Edition

ISBN:

Acknowledgments & Credits

This book would not have been possible without the inspiration, encouragement, and support of many people.

To everyone who shared their stories, perspectives, and insights—thank you. Your honesty and courage illuminate the path to understanding and reconciliation.

To the friends, colleagues, and community members who engaged in thoughtful conversations, challenged assumptions, and modeled compassion in action—your presence made this work stronger and more meaningful.

To the countless peacemakers—past and present—who have shown us what it means to forgive, to listen, and to lead with empathy, this book is dedicated in part to you.

Finally, to every reader who believes in the possibility of healing and chooses to build bridges rather than walls—thank you for walking this journey.

May this book be a small step toward the greater work we are all called to do.

Because, truly, we are not enemies. We never were.

Contents

Author's Note 1

Introduction: The Path to Understanding 3

Chapter 1 - The Roots of Conflict 5

Chapter 2 - The Power of Listening 9

Chapter 3 - Finding Strength in Vulnerability 13

Chapter 4 - The Art of Forgiveness 17

Chapter 5 - Building Bridges for the Future 21

Chapter 6 - The Role of Apologies in Reconciliation 25

Chapter 7 - The Science of Human Connection 29

Chapter 8 - Conflict Resolution in Professional Environments 33

Chapter 9 - How Different Cultures Handle Conflict 37

Chapter 10 - Recognizing Toxic Group Mentalities 41

Chapter 11 - Overcoming Fear and Prejudice 45

Chapter 12 - Practical Strategies for Reconciliation 49

Chapter 13 - The Ongoing Journey of Reconciliation 55

Conclusion - We Are Not Enemies After All 59

Author's Note

I wrote this book because I have seen firsthand how misunderstandings, unhealed wounds, and deep-seated divisions tear relationships apart.

I have watched families stop speaking over differences that could have been resolved. I have seen workplaces become hostile environments because no one knew how to handle conflict constructively.

I have observed communities and entire nations grow increasingly polarized, driven by fear, misinformation, and the belief that those who disagree with us must be our enemies.

But I have also seen the power of reconciliation. I have witnessed moments where a simple conversation healed years of resentment. I have experienced the transformation that comes from listening—really listening—to someone whose perspective is different from my own.

And I have learned that conflict, when approached with the right mindset, is not a dead end but an opportunity for growth and deeper connection.

This book is my attempt to share what I've learned. It is an invitation to challenge the idea that we must be divided and to explore a different path—one of understanding, patience, and bridge-building.

If you have ever struggled with a broken relationship, a difficult conversation, or the weight of division, I hope this book serves as a guide and a source of hope.

Because the truth is, we are not enemies. We never were.

Introduction

The Path to Understanding

Conflict is as old as humanity itself. It arises in families, workplaces, communities, and even within nations. Some conflicts are small and fleeting, while others deepen into long-standing divisions. When left unresolved, these divisions become wounds that separate us, making true connection seem impossible.

But what if conflict wasn't the end of the road? What if it was a doorway to something greater—a deeper understanding, a stronger bond, a path toward unity?

This book is about breaking the cycle of division. It's about shifting our perspective from opposition to opportunity, from resentment to resolution.

It is not about avoiding conflict, but rather learning how to navigate it in a way that builds rather than destroys.

Through history, psychology, real-world stories, and practical tools, this book will help you:

- Understand why conflicts arise and how they escalate.
- Learn the power of listening and empathy in resolving disputes.
- Break free from toxic group mentalities and echo chambers.
- Develop strategies for forgiveness, reconciliation, and bridge-building.

This is not just a book about conflict—it is a guide to transforming relationships, communities, and even societies.

If you have ever felt the weight of a broken relationship, the sting of betrayal, or the frustration of division, this book is for you.

Because, after all, we are not enemies. We never were.

Chapter 1

The Roots of Conflict

Conflict is a natural part of human interactions. It arises from misunderstandings, unmet expectations, opposing beliefs, and personal or cultural differences. While conflict is often seen as negative, it can also be an opportunity for growth and deeper understanding—if approached with the right mindset.

1.1 Understanding the Origins of Conflict

The roots of conflict can be traced to multiple factors, including:

1. Miscommunication – A lack of clarity or misunderstanding can quickly escalate minor disagreements.
2. Differing Values and Beliefs – People have diverse perspectives shaped by culture, upbringing, and experiences.

3. Unmet Needs and Expectations – When individuals feel ignored, undervalued, or taken for granted, conflicts emerge.

4. Power Struggles – Whether in personal relationships, workplaces, or politics, power imbalances can create tension.

5. Historical and Cultural Divides – Past grievances and generational conflicts influence how people react in the present.

1.2 Case Study: The Impact of Miscommunication

Consider two coworkers, Jake and Maria, who are collaborating on a project. Jake believes Maria is ignoring his input, while Maria assumes Jake is uninterested because he hasn't voiced strong opinions. The truth? Maria values consensus, waiting for Jake to take the lead, while Jake, hesitant to interrupt, remains silent. This misunderstanding nearly leads to a conflict—until they engage in an open conversation.

1.3 Psychological Triggers of Conflict

Neuroscientists have found that when we feel threatened—physically or emotionally—our brain's amygdala activates the "fight-or-flight" response. This can cause people to react defensively rather than engage in constructive dialogue.

- Fear-based reactions: Some conflicts stem from deep-seated fears, such as rejection, failure, or loss of control.
- Ego and pride: The need to "win" an argument or prove oneself right can prolong unnecessary disputes.
- Assumptions and biases: Preconceived notions about a person or situation can distort reality, fueling unnecessary tensions.

1.4 How Historical Conflicts Shape Modern Disputes

History provides numerous examples of conflicts rooted in long-standing grievances:

- The Cold War: A prolonged ideological and geopolitical conflict driven by fear, competition, and misunderstandings.
- Family Feuds: Many families experience long-term estrangements because of past arguments left unresolved.
- Workplace Conflicts: Generational gaps between employees often lead to workplace culture clashes.

1.5 Turning Conflict into Opportunity

Understanding the roots of conflict allows us to respond rather than react. By recognizing triggers and underlying causes, individuals and communities can work towards constructive solutions.

Key approaches include:

- ✓ Active listening – Seeking to understand rather than immediately refute.
- ✓ Empathy and perspective-taking – Stepping into the other person's shoes.
- ✓ Clear communication – Expressing thoughts and feelings openly, reducing assumptions.
- ✓ Collaborative problem-solving – Working towards a win-win rather than a win-lose scenario.

1.6 Final Thoughts

Conflicts are inevitable, but how we manage and resolve them determines whether they divide or strengthen us. In the next chapter, we will explore the power of listening, one of the most effective tools for de-escalating conflict and fostering understanding.

Chapter 2

The Power of Listening

One of the most powerful yet overlooked tools in conflict resolution is listening. Many conflicts arise not because of disagreements but because people feel unheard. True listening fosters understanding, diffuses tension, and paves the way for reconciliation.

2.1 Why Listening Matters

When we listen actively, we:

1. Acknowledge the other person's perspective – People are more willing to engage in a dialogue when they feel respected.

2. Reduce misunderstandings – Many conflicts are rooted in misinterpretations that could have been avoided through effective listening.

3. Create emotional safety – Feeling heard and validated reduces defensiveness, making open communication possible.

2.2 The Difference Between Hearing and Listening

- Hearing is passive; it involves perceiving sound but not fully processing it.
- Listening is active; it requires attention, interpretation, and response.

Consider a conversation between a manager and an employee. If the manager simply hears complaints without acknowledging or responding to concerns, the employee may feel dismissed, leading to resentment. However, if the manager listens attentively and asks clarifying questions, the employee feels valued, reducing the chance of conflict.

2.3 Barriers to Effective Listening

Despite its importance, many people struggle with listening. Some common barriers include:

○ Interrupting – Jumping in before the other person has finished speaking.

○ Thinking about what to say next – Instead of focusing on the speaker's words.

○ Judging – Making assumptions about the speaker before they finish.

- Distractions – Allowing phones, external noise, or personal thoughts to interfere.

2.4 The Art of Active Listening

Active listening involves fully engaging with the speaker through:

- ✓ Eye contact – Showing attentiveness without intimidation.
- ✓ Nonverbal cues – Nodding, leaning in, and maintaining an open posture.
- ✓ Reflective responses – Repeating or paraphrasing what was said to confirm understanding.
- ✓ Asking open-ended questions – Encouraging deeper discussion.
- ✓ Avoiding defensive reactions – Focusing on the speaker's message rather than planning a rebuttal.

2.5 Case Study: Resolving a Conflict Through Listening

Emma and David, longtime friends, had a falling out due to a misunderstanding. Emma felt that David was ignoring her, while David believed Emma had been distant. Months passed without either reaching out. Finally, they sat down to talk. Instead of blaming each other, they practiced active listening, expressing their feelings without interruption. They discovered that both had been struggling with personal issues and had misinterpreted the other's behavior. Their friendship was restored through listening.

2.6 Listening in High-Stress Situations

Conflicts are most challenging when emotions run high. During heated discussions:

1. Take a pause – A moment of silence can prevent impulsive reactions.
2. Validate emotions – Even if you disagree, acknowledge how the other person feels.
3. Clarify intentions – Ask, "What do you mean by that?" instead of assuming the worst.
4. Use neutral language – Avoid accusatory phrases like "You always" or "You never."

2.7 Listening as a Path to Reconciliation

Great leaders, mediators, and diplomats understand that listening is a tool for peace.

By listening, we:

🌱 Strengthen relationships – People trust those who truly listen.

🌱 Encourage honest dialogue – Open discussions lead to solutions.

🌱 Defuse hostility – Feeling heard reduces anger and resentment.

2.8 Final Thoughts

Listening is not about agreeing; it is about understanding. Many conflicts persist because individuals refuse to hear each other out. In the next chapter, we will explore how vulnerability can be a strength rather than a weakness when resolving disputes.

Chapter 3

Finding Strength in Vulnerability

Vulnerability is often perceived as a weakness, but in reality, it is one of the most powerful tools for building trust, resolving conflict, and fostering deeper connections. When we allow ourselves to be open and authentic, we invite understanding and create space for healing.

3.1 Why Vulnerability is a Strength

Vulnerability means being honest about our fears, mistakes, and emotions.

It allows for:

✓ Genuine connection – People relate more to authenticity than perfection.

- ✓ Conflict resolution – Admitting when we are wrong defuses defensiveness.
- ✓ Personal growth – Acknowledging our struggles helps us overcome them.

3.2 Breaking the Fear of Vulnerability

Many people avoid vulnerability because of:

○ Fear of rejection – Worrying that openness will lead to judgment.

○ Fear of appearing weak – Believing that emotions signal fragility.

○ Past trauma – Negative experiences make trust difficult.

Yet, avoiding vulnerability often worsens conflict. When we build walls to protect ourselves, we also block opportunities for understanding.

3.3 Case Study: The Power of Openness in Conflict Resolution

John and Lisa had been married for ten years, but resentment had built up due to unresolved issues. Whenever disagreements arose, they deflected emotions rather than expressing them. During a counseling session, John admitted, "I feel like I'm failing as a husband." Lisa, shocked by his honesty, replied, "I never knew you felt that way. I've been scared that you don't care." This moment of vulnerability shifted their relationship, leading to productive conversations and emotional healing.

3.4 How to Embrace Vulnerability in Conflict

1. Acknowledge your emotions – Instead of suppressing feelings, recognize them.
2. Use "I" statements – Express how you feel without blaming others ("I feel unheard" vs. "You never listen").
3. Admit mistakes – Apologizing and taking responsibility fosters mutual respect.
4. Allow others to be vulnerable – Respond with empathy rather than criticism.
5. Seek to understand, not just defend – Instead of preparing counterarguments, focus on the other person's perspective.

3.5 The Role of Empathy in Vulnerability

Empathy is the bridge that makes vulnerability safe. When we listen with compassion, we create an environment where people feel comfortable expressing themselves.

— Empathy says: "I hear you. I see you. Your feelings are valid."

— Judgment says: "You're too emotional. Get over it."

A workplace study showed that teams with empathetic leaders had higher productivity and lower turnover rates. When employees felt safe being open about challenges, they collaborated more effectively.

3.6 Vulnerability in Leadership and Mediation

Great leaders and mediators embrace vulnerability:

- ✓ Nelson Mandela – His willingness to forgive and openly discuss his pain helped unite South Africa.
- ✓ Abraham Lincoln – He acknowledged his struggles and sought input from critics, strengthening his leadership.
- ✓ Therapists and counselors – They create safe spaces by being approachable and empathetic.

3.7 Final Thoughts

Vulnerability is not about weakness—it is about courage. When we allow ourselves to be open, we invite trust, healing, and deeper connections.

In the next chapter, we will explore how forgiveness plays a crucial role in reconciliation .

Chapter 4

The Art of Forgiveness

Forgiveness is one of the most misunderstood yet transformative acts in conflict resolution. Many see it as a sign of weakness or as excusing harmful behavior. In truth, forgiveness is a powerful tool for healing—not just for the one being forgiven, but especially for the one who forgives.

4.1 What Forgiveness Is—and Isn't

Forgiveness is:

- ✓ Letting go of resentment – Releasing the grip that anger and pain have on your life.
- ✓ Choosing peace over bitterness – Prioritizing your mental and emotional wellbeing.
- ✓ A journey, not a one-time decision – It often takes time and effort.

Forgiveness is NOT:

🚫 Excusing harmful behavior – You can forgive someone without condoning their actions.

🚫 Forgetting – It's about remembering without allowing the memory to control you.

🚫 Reconciling automatically – Forgiveness can happen without restoring the relationship.

4.2 The Psychological Benefits of Forgiveness

Studies have shown that people who practice forgiveness experience:

- Lower levels of stress and anxiety
- Reduced symptoms of depression
- Improved cardiovascular health
- Stronger interpersonal relationships

When we hold onto anger and resentment, we carry a mental and emotional burden that can be toxic over time.

4.3 Personal Story: Forgiving a Betrayal

After years of friendship, Monica discovered her best friend had spread rumors about her. For months, Monica avoided her, consumed by betrayal. But the anger began to affect her sleep, work, and other relationships. Eventually, she wrote a letter—not to be sent, but to express her pain and forgive her friend internally. That act freed her from the emotional chains of resentment.

4.4 Steps Toward Forgiveness

1. Acknowledge the pain – Don't minimize your emotions.
2. Decide to forgive – It's a choice that may require reaffirmation.
3. Understand the other person's humanity – Even good people make harmful mistakes.
4. Release the expectation of an apology – Sometimes closure comes from within.
5. Focus on your healing – Forgiveness is more about your freedom than theirs.

4.5 The Power of Self-Forgiveness

Often, the hardest person to forgive is ourselves. We replay our past mistakes, judge ourselves harshly, and struggle with shame. But self-forgiveness is essential to personal growth and healthy relationships.

Self-forgiveness involves:

- Taking responsibility without self-condemnation
- Making amends when possible
- Accepting that we are not defined by our worst moments

4.6 Forgiveness in Communities and Nations

Entire communities and nations have used forgiveness to rebuild after deep wounds.

- South Africa's Truth and Reconciliation Commission allowed victims and perpetrators to share their stories and seek forgiveness.

- Rwandan reconciliation efforts after the 1994 genocide brought communities back together despite unimaginable pain.

These efforts demonstrate that forgiveness is possible even in the most extreme circumstances.

4.7 Final Thoughts

Forgiveness is not a gift to the offender—it is a gift to yourself. By choosing to forgive, you take back control of your emotions and make space for healing.

In the next chapter, we will explore how to build bridges for the future, even after relationships have been strained or broken.

Chapter 5

Building Bridges for the Future

Forgiveness and understanding are essential, but they're only part of the journey. To truly heal and grow beyond conflict, we must actively build bridges. Bridge-building is about restoring trust, nurturing connection, and creating shared futures, even with those we've disagreed with.

5.1 Why Building Bridges Matters

Once forgiveness is offered or reconciliation begins, many ask, "What next?" This chapter explores how to transform a moment of peace into a sustained relationship.

Bridge-building allows for:

- ✓ Long-term connection – Not just resolving the past, but nurturing a better future.
- ✓ Prevention of future conflicts – Creating understanding reduces the risk of repeated mistakes.
- ✓ Strengthening communities – Unified relationships contribute to healthier societies.

5.2 The Principles of Bridge-Building

1. Mutual respect – Valuing the dignity and worth of the other person.
2. Consistent communication – Staying in touch and clarifying intentions regularly.
3. Shared goals – Identifying common interests that benefit both parties.
4. Willingness to compromise – Letting go of perfection to find workable solutions.
5. Patience and persistence – Rebuilding takes time and intentional effort.

5.3 Case Study: Restoring a Broken Business Partnership

Andre and Malik co-owned a small marketing firm. After a disagreement over finances, their relationship soured, and the business suffered. Months later, they met with a mediator. Both acknowledged mistakes and committed to transparent communication. Over time, they redefined their roles, implemented regular check-ins, and reestablished trust. Their business recovered—and so did their friendship.

5.4 Tools for Practical Bridge-Building

- Regular check-ins – Schedule ongoing conversations, especially after resolving a conflict.
- Community dialogues – Host forums or discussion circles to share experiences and listen.
- Written agreements – In professional or formal settings, clarify expectations to avoid future misunderstandings.
- Acts of service – Demonstrate goodwill through kindness and support.
- Education and awareness – Learn about each other's backgrounds, cultures, and perspectives.

5.5 Reconciliation vs. Restoration

Not all relationships will return to what they were before. Sometimes the goal is not to go back, but to build something new. Reconciliation is about peace. Restoration is about closeness. It's okay if only one is possible.

- Example: Two former friends may reconcile by forgiving each other but choose not to reenter a close friendship.
- Example: A divided community may come together to build shared spaces even if ideological differences remain.

5.6 Bridge-Building on a Societal Scale

- Post-conflict nations often hold peace talks, truth commissions, and social campaigns to foster healing.

- Religious and interfaith organizations collaborate across differences to address poverty, injustice, and social needs.

- Grassroots movements led by youth, artists, and educators open space for dialogue and action.

5.7 Final Thoughts

Building bridges is not a passive process. It requires courage, vision, and a commitment to growth.

Each time we choose dialogue over division, we create a better future—not only for ourselves but for generations to come.

In the next chapter, we will explore the role of apologies in reconciliation, and how a sincere "I'm sorry" can become a turning point in even the most difficult relationships.

Chapter 6

The Role of Apologies in Reconciliation

A sincere apology has the power to open hearts, close old wounds, and reset relationships. Yet many people find it difficult to apologize genuinely, often fearing it shows weakness or guilt. In truth, a heartfelt apology is a powerful act of strength, humility, and emotional intelligence.

6.1 Why Apologies Matter

Apologies play a critical role in repairing harm and rebuilding trust. They:

— Validate the other person's experience

— Acknowledge responsibility

— Demonstrate accountability and maturity

— Lay the groundwork for forgiveness and healing

Without an apology, even minor offenses can fester into deep resentment.

6.2 Elements of a Genuine Apology

A real apology is more than just saying "I'm sorry." It includes:

1. Acknowledgment – Naming the specific harm caused.

   Example: "I realize I hurt you when I interrupted you during the meeting."

2. Responsibility – Owning your actions without excuses.

   Not: "I'm sorry you were offended." But: "I'm sorry I said something offensive."

3. Remorse – Showing sincere regret.

   "I feel terrible for how I made you feel."

4. Restitution – Offering to make things right.

   "What can I do to repair the damage?"

5. Commitment to change – Stating how you'll avoid repeating the mistake.

   "I'll be more mindful of my words moving forward."

6.3 What Apologies Are Not

- They're not manipulative tools to force forgiveness.
- They're not performance pieces for public approval.
- They're not vague or deflective ("Mistakes were made" isn't an apology).

- They're not rushed – A real apology comes after reflection, not pressure.

6.4 Case Study: Healing a Workplace Rift

Two coworkers, Elena and Marcus, had a fallout over miscommunication that led to a failed presentation. Tensions lingered for weeks. Eventually, Marcus approached Elena and said, "I didn't take your input seriously, and I see now that it hurt the team. I'm really sorry for that." His sincerity surprised Elena and melted her defensiveness. It was the beginning of a renewed working relationship.

6.5 The Risk—and Reward—of Apologizing First

Apologizing first often feels unfair, especially when both parties are at fault. But doing so:

- Breaks the cycle of pride and defensiveness
- Opens the door for reciprocal vulnerability
- Demonstrates leadership and emotional maturity

Even if the other person doesn't respond immediately, your apology plants a seed for future reconciliation.

6.6 Cultural and Social Contexts of Apology

In some cultures, apologies are frequent and expected. In others, they're rare and may be seen as shameful. It's important to understand the cultural lens through which apologies are given and received.

- In Japanese culture, formal apologies are essential and often ritualized.

- In some Western contexts, admitting fault can carry legal or professional risks, making apologies more complex.

Understanding these nuances fosters empathy in cross-cultural relationships.

6.7 When an Apology Isn't Enough

Sometimes, words alone aren't sufficient—especially in situations involving deep betrayal or systemic harm. In those cases:

- Consistent actions over time are required to rebuild trust.
- Listening without defensiveness is often more healing than speaking.
- Being patient with the timeline of forgiveness is essential.

6.8 Final Thoughts

Apologizing is an act of courage. It requires vulnerability, empathy, and self-awareness. While it cannot erase the past, it can powerfully influence the future.

In the next chapter, we'll explore the science of human connection and how we're biologically wired for empathy, cooperation, and reconciliation.

Chapter 7

The Science of Human Connection

At the heart of every conflict—and every resolution—is a relationship. Science reveals that human beings are biologically wired for connection. We thrive when we feel safe, understood, and supported. Understanding the neuroscience and psychology behind human connection helps us build healthier relationships and resolve conflict more effectively.

7.1 The Biology of Connection

The brain is a social organ. Studies show that meaningful human interaction activates regions associated with reward, safety, and empathy.

- Oxytocin, known as the "bonding hormone," is released during positive social interactions. It promotes trust and reduces stress.

- The mirror neuron system in our brains helps us empathize by internally mirroring others' emotional states.
- Cortisol, the stress hormone, decreases when we feel socially supported and increases during prolonged conflict or isolation.

7.2 The Role of Empathy

Empathy is the cornerstone of connection. It allows us to sense, feel, and understand the emotions of others—even when we don't agree with them.

There are three types of empathy:

1. Cognitive empathy – Understanding what someone else is thinking.
2. Emotional empathy – Feeling what someone else is feeling.
3. Compassionate empathy – Wanting to help based on what the other person is experiencing.

Practicing empathy helps us approach conflicts with curiosity instead of judgment.

7.3 Case Study: Empathy in Mediation

In a community dispute over zoning laws, residents were angry with city officials. Instead of presenting data or defending policies, the mediator began the meeting by asking, "Can someone tell me how this decision is affecting your life?" One resident shared their fear of losing their family home. That moment of vulnerability shifted the tone of the conversation. The officials began listening—and empathy became the bridge to compromise.

7.4 Loneliness, Disconnection, and Conflict

Social disconnection is a public health issue. Studies have shown that loneliness can be as harmful as smoking 15 cigarettes a day. People who feel isolated are more likely to:

- Experience anxiety and depression
- Be suspicious or hostile in relationships
- Have reduced capacity for empathy

When people feel disconnected, they're more prone to misinterpret others' actions and engage in conflict.

7.5 Strengthening Connection in Daily Life

We can boost human connection in our lives and communities by:

- Listening with presence – Give undivided attention, without distractions.
- Practicing gratitude – Express appreciation to others regularly.
- Being vulnerable – Share feelings and personal experiences.
- Engaging in shared experiences – Participate in activities that bring people together.
- Checking in – Ask others how they're really doing, and be prepared to listen.

7.6 Technology and Human Connection

While technology connects us more than ever, it can also contribute to superficial relationships. Texting lacks tone, social media can create echo chambers, and constant connectivity can lead to burnout.

Healthy tech use includes:

- Prioritizing in-person or video conversations for important matters
- Taking breaks from screens to engage in real-world interactions
- Being intentional about how we use online platforms to foster connection rather than division

7.7 Final Thoughts

Science confirms what we already sense: we are not meant to live—or resolve conflict—in isolation. The more connected we feel, the more capable we are of navigating challenges with compassion, patience, and perspective.

In the next chapter, we'll explore how to apply these insights in professional environments, where tensions can arise but resolution is always possible.

Chapter 8

Conflict Resolution in Professional Environments

Conflict is inevitable in any workplace. Differences in personalities, communication styles, roles, and responsibilities often lead to tension. But professional environments also offer structured opportunities to resolve disagreements effectively—when handled with intention and care.

8.1 Why Workplace Conflict Happens

Common sources of workplace conflict include:

- Miscommunication – Lack of clarity in roles, expectations, or tone.

- Competing priorities – Teams working toward different goals without alignment.
- Cultural differences – Differing approaches to authority, time, and collaboration.
- Power dynamics – Disagreements over leadership, recognition, or decision-making.

8.2 The Cost of Unresolved Conflict

When left unchecked, workplace conflict can result in:

- Lower productivity
- Increased absenteeism
- High employee turnover
- Poor morale and team cohesion
- Damaged company reputation

8.3 Principles of Professional Conflict Resolution

- Address conflict early – Don't wait for issues to grow.
- Maintain professionalism – Separate the person from the problem.
- Use neutral language – Avoid accusatory or inflammatory phrasing.
- Seek clarity – Ask questions instead of making assumptions.
- Stay solution-focused – Prioritize outcomes that benefit the team.

8.4 Case Study: A Cross-Team Disagreement

A product development team clashed with the sales team over delivery timelines. Sales accused developers of delays; developers blamed sales for unrealistic promises. The manager brought both groups together for a structured discussion. Each side explained their challenges. Together, they created a shared timeline that accounted for both perspectives. Tensions eased, and future collaboration improved.

8.5 The Role of Managers and HR

Leaders have a responsibility to:

- Model respectful conflict resolution
- Provide regular training on communication and feedback
- Intervene impartially when disputes arise
- Create a culture where speaking up is safe

HR departments can help mediate conflicts, investigate serious grievances, and design systems that support healthy team dynamics.

8.6 Techniques for Resolving Workplace Conflict

- Active listening – Allow each person to share their view without interruption.
- Restating concerns – Repeat what you've heard to ensure clarity and show you understand.
- Acknowledging impact – Even if unintentional, recognize how actions affected others.

- Collaborative problem-solving – Brainstorm solutions together rather than assigning blame.

- Follow-up plans – Agree on next steps and accountability checks.

8.7 Embracing Diversity and Inclusion

Diverse workplaces bring unique strengths but also new challenges. Conflict may arise due to unconscious bias or cultural misunderstandings. Inclusive conflict resolution:

- Honors different communication styles

- Encourages equity in decision-making

- Challenges harmful assumptions

- Celebrates learning through difference

8.8 Final Thoughts

Conflict in professional environments doesn't have to be destructive. With the right mindset and tools, it can become a catalyst for innovation, understanding, and stronger teams. Organizations that embrace constructive conflict resolution are more adaptable, resilient, and successful.

In the next chapter, we'll examine how different cultures approach conflict , and what we can learn from their wisdom and practices.

Chapter 9

How Different Cultures Handle Conflict

Conflict is a universal human experience, but how we handle it varies greatly across cultures. Understanding these differences can prevent misunderstandings, build empathy, and enhance our ability to resolve disputes in a diverse world.

9.1 Cultural Approaches to Conflict

Different cultures approach conflict with varying degrees of directness, formality, and emotional expression. These approaches generally fall into two broad categories:

1. High-context cultures (e.g., Japan, China, Arab countries):

— Communication is indirect and nuanced.

— Preserving harmony and saving face are priorities.

- Conflict is often addressed subtly or through intermediaries.

2. Low-context cultures (e.g., U.S., Germany, Australia):

- Communication is direct and explicit.

- Openness and transparency are valued.

- Conflict is usually addressed head-on and quickly.

Neither approach is better—just different. Problems arise when individuals from these cultures interact without understanding one another's style.

9.2 Case Study: A Multinational Project Team

An American manager grew frustrated with her Japanese colleague, who never provided firm answers in meetings. The Japanese colleague, in turn, found the manager aggressive and disrespectful. After a facilitated conversation, both learned their styles were culturally influenced—not personal. This awareness helped them adapt and collaborate more effectively.

9.3 Emotion and Expression

- In Mediterranean and Latin cultures, emotional expression is often passionate and open.

- In East Asian cultures, emotional restraint is valued, especially in public or professional settings.

This difference can lead to misunderstandings. A quiet response might be interpreted as disengagement in one culture but as respect in another.

9.4 Conflict Avoidance vs. Confrontation

— Some cultures see confrontation as disrespectful and avoid it at all costs.

— Others view it as healthy and necessary for progress.

Understanding these perspectives helps us reframe how we interpret others' behavior.

9.5 Building Cross-Cultural Competence

To navigate cultural differences in conflict:

— Stay curious — Ask questions rather than assume.

— Listen actively — Tune into what is said and how it's said.

— Adjust your communication style — Match tone and formality to your audience.

— Avoid ethnocentrism — Don't judge other cultures based on your own norms.

— Learn cultural histories — Context helps explain behavior and beliefs.

9.6 Global Business and Diplomacy

Cross-cultural conflict resolution is essential in international business and politics. Diplomats, CEOs, and peace negotiators often undergo training in intercultural communication to avoid blunders and build trust.

— Missteps, such as refusing a gift in some cultures or demanding eye contact in others, can create conflict unintentionally.

— Cultural awareness enables more respectful and effective dialogue.

9.7 Final Thoughts

Culture shapes not only what we say, but how we say it, and what we consider respectful or offensive. By learning from diverse approaches to conflict, we expand our toolkit for understanding and harmony.

In the next chapter, we'll explore how to recognize and resist toxic group mentalities that often fuel division and conflict in communities and organizations.

Chapter 10

Recognizing Toxic Group Mentalities

Group loyalty can be a powerful force for good—but it can also lead to dangerous thinking when taken to extremes. Toxic group mentalities develop when allegiance to the group overrides empathy, logic, or ethical behavior. Recognizing and resisting these dynamics is critical to preventing conflict and division.

10.1 What Is a Toxic Group Mentality?

A toxic group mentality occurs when a group:

- Discourages critical thinking
- Demands absolute loyalty
- Demonizes outsiders or dissenters
- Promotes an "us vs. them" worldview

- Justifies harmful behavior for the sake of the group's goals

These patterns show up in political parties, religious sects, social movements, workplaces, and even families.

10.2 Psychological Drivers Behind Groupthink

1. Need for belonging – Humans are social creatures who fear exclusion.
2. Fear of rejection – Speaking out against the group can lead to isolation or punishment.
3. Echo chambers – When people surround themselves only with those who agree, beliefs become more extreme.
4. Authority pressure – Leaders who discourage questioning create rigid, dogmatic environments.

10.3 Case Study: A Workplace Culture Gone Wrong

A company known for high performance rewarded only the most aggressive salespeople. Over time, unethical behavior became normalized, and those who questioned it were ostracized. The company eventually faced a major scandal. Toxic group loyalty had blinded the team to their own values and accountability.

10.4 Red Flags to Watch For

- Group discourages debate or open discussion
- People feel unsafe expressing differing opinions
- Members repeat slogans instead of forming independent thoughts

- Leaders are seen as infallible or above criticism
- Dissent is punished or shamed

10.5 How to Resist Toxic Group Influence

- Think critically – Ask questions and evaluate information independently.
- Diversify input – Seek out voices from outside the group to broaden perspective.
- Stay grounded in values – Be clear on your principles and let them guide your decisions.
- Encourage dissent – Value disagreement as a tool for growth and clarity.
- Support whistleblowers – Protect those who speak up about injustice or wrongdoing.

10.6 Social Media and Group Mentality

Online platforms intensify groupthink. Algorithms reward outrage and polarization, and users often fall into echo chambers. Online "cancel culture," mob mentality, and viral misinformation thrive in these environments.

To navigate social media:

- Pause before sharing inflammatory content
- Fact-check sources
- Follow people with diverse views

– Reflect before reacting

10.7 Healing from Group Harm

Leaving a toxic group can be painful and disorienting. Those who exit often experience grief, guilt, and loneliness. Healing involves:

– Finding new communities rooted in respect

– Reclaiming one's voice and critical thinking

– Processing the emotional impact with support

10.8 Final Thoughts

Toxic group mentalities thrive on fear and conformity. Healthy groups encourage integrity, diversity, and accountability. By recognizing warning signs and prioritizing our shared humanity over blind loyalty, we create space for dialogue, empathy, and lasting peace.

In the next chapter, we'll explore how to overcome fear and prejudice, which often lie at the root of group division and misunderstanding.

Chapter 11

Overcoming Fear and Prejudice

Fear and prejudice are two of the most powerful drivers of conflict. They distort reality, fuel hostility, and create unnecessary barriers between people. To foster reconciliation, we must learn how to identify and confront these forces in ourselves and in the world around us.

11.1 Understanding the Roots of Fear

Fear is a natural response to the unknown or perceived threats. It becomes harmful when it:

- Causes irrational behavior
- Justifies discrimination or violence
- Prevents open communication

- Reinforces stereotypes and "us vs. them" thinking

Fear thrives in uncertainty, misinformation, and isolation. It narrows our worldview and increases the likelihood of conflict.

11.2 Prejudice: Learned, Not Innate

Prejudice is a preconceived opinion not based on reason or actual experience. It is often learned from:

- Cultural narratives
- Family and peer influence
- Media portrayals
- Historical trauma

Prejudice isn't always obvious. It can manifest in subtle assumptions, biases, and behaviors. Recognizing it requires self-awareness and humility.

11.3 Case Study: A Community Divided

In a small town, a refugee family moved into a neighborhood with little exposure to immigration. Some residents, fueled by fear-based media coverage, became suspicious and distant. One neighbor, curious rather than fearful, invited the family for dinner. That gesture led to friendships, shared understanding, and a gradual shift in community attitudes.

11.4 How Fear and Prejudice Spread

1. Stereotyping – Reducing individuals to simplistic traits.

2. Scapegoating – Blaming a person or group for broader problems.
3. Dehumanization – Viewing others as "less than" or dangerous.
4. Group conformity – Going along with prejudiced ideas to fit in.
5. Polarized media – Spreading narratives that reinforce fear and division.

11.5 Strategies to Overcome Fear and Prejudice

- Educate yourself – Learn about different cultures, histories, and experiences.
- Expose yourself to diversity – Seek out interactions with people unlike yourself.
- Challenge your assumptions – Ask, "Why do I believe this?" or "Where did I learn this?"
- Have courageous conversations – Talk openly about differences with respect.
- Practice empathy – Put yourself in someone else's shoes.

11.6 The Role of Leaders and Institutions

Leaders in education, politics, religion, and media play a powerful role in shaping beliefs. Inclusive leadership:

- Models empathy and openness
- Condemns bigotry and misinformation
- Builds policies that promote equity and justice

When institutions stand up against prejudice, they create safer environments for all.

11.7 Healing Historical Fear and Prejudice

Many conflicts are rooted in historical injustices—colonialism, slavery, war, genocide. Acknowledging these histories and creating space for truth-telling and healing is essential to reconciliation.

- Truth commissions, public apologies, reparations, and education reform help address generational wounds.
- Interfaith and intercultural dialogues build trust where division once reigned.

11.8 Final Thoughts

Fear and prejudice shrink our world. Overcoming them expands it. It requires curiosity, compassion, and the willingness to step outside our comfort zones. As we learn to see each other fully and fairly, we create space for peace, connection, and true reconciliation.

In the next chapter, we'll explore practical, everyday strategies for reconciliation —how to move from intention to action in healing relationships and communities.

Chapter 12

Practical Strategies for Reconciliation

Reconciliation is more than a concept—it's a commitment to healing and moving forward. It requires more than good intentions; it calls for consistent, compassionate action. Whether in personal relationships or divided communities, practical steps can turn hope into tangible change.

12.1 What Reconciliation Looks Like

Reconciliation doesn't always mean returning to how things were. It might mean:

— Establishing new boundaries

— Building a new kind of relationship

— Agreeing to disagree peacefully

- Creating mutual understanding without full agreement

Reconciliation is not about erasing the past—it's about reimagining the future.

12.2 Step-by-Step Framework for Reconciliation

1. Preparation

- Reflect on what happened and what you hope to achieve.
- Check your emotions and readiness to engage respectfully.
- Clarify your intentions—do you want peace, closure, repair?

2. Initiate Dialogue

- Reach out respectfully.
- Choose a neutral time and place.
- Set expectations for openness and active listening.

3. Tell the Truth

- Share your perspective honestly, using "I" statements.
- Listen without interrupting or correcting.
- Validate each other's emotions and experiences.

4. Take Responsibility

- Acknowledge harm done, even if unintentional.
- Apologize sincerely, without excuses or conditions.
- Allow space for the other person's reaction.

5. Work Toward Repair

- Ask, "What do you need to move forward?"
- Offer concrete ways to rebuild trust.
- Set shared agreements or goals.

6. Follow Through

- Rebuilding trust takes time—be consistent.
- Check in regularly and revisit the conversation if needed.
- Show through your actions that you're committed to change.

12.3 Everyday Reconciliation Practices

- Active listening – Create space for others to feel heard.
- Small acts of kindness – Repair trust with simple, thoughtful gestures.
- Assume positive intent – Choose empathy before judgment.
- Speak up for peace – Challenge harmful rhetoric in your circles.
- Model reconciliation – Be a peacemaker in your home, work, and community.

12.4 Reconciliation in Communities

Communities can foster reconciliation by:

- Hosting public dialogues and healing circles
- Supporting restorative justice initiatives
- Offering counseling or mediation services
- Celebrating diverse cultures and histories
- Partnering across divides for shared goals

12.5 Case Study: A Neighborhood Initiative

In a racially divided neighborhood, tensions rose after a high-profile incident. Local leaders launched a weekly "Dialogue on the Porch" series, inviting neighbors to share stories, fears, and hopes. Over months, mistrust gave way to understanding. The initiative sparked community projects, joint advocacy, and lasting friendships.

12.6 Obstacles to Reconciliation

- Unhealed trauma – Some wounds require professional support to process.
- Lack of accountability – True reconciliation can't occur without responsibility.
- Unequal effort – Both parties must be willing, though effort may look different.

- Outside interference – Gossip, misinformation, or political agendas can derail progress.

12.7 Final Thoughts

Reconciliation is a process, not a destination. It's made possible through humility, courage, and love in action. Even small steps—one conversation, one act of kindness—can restore what was broken. When we each commit to reconciliation, we become architects of a more compassionate world.

In the final chapter, we'll reflect on the ongoing journey of reconciliation and how we can keep walking this path together.

We Are Not Enemies After All

Chapter 13

The Ongoing Journey of Reconciliation

Reconciliation is not a single event or a one-time achievement—it is a lifelong journey. Relationships grow, change, and sometimes face setbacks. The work of healing, understanding, and building connection must be sustained over time, both personally and collectively.

13.1 Reconciliation as a Daily Practice

Just as we brush our teeth daily or exercise to stay healthy, reconciliation thrives through regular, intentional actions:

— Choosing patience over pride

— Listening when it's hard

— Owning our mistakes quickly

— Rebuilding trust even after disappointment

These everyday practices prevent old wounds from reopening and help us grow stronger through conflict.

13.2 Embracing Imperfection

No reconciliation journey is perfect. Misunderstandings happen. Emotions rise again. Progress is not always linear.

What matters is the commitment to come back to the table, again and again.

— Forgiveness may need to be repeated.

— Apologies may need to be deepened.

— Boundaries may need to be adjusted.

Staying on the path matters more than walking it perfectly.

13.3 Case Study: A Family's Continued Healing

After years of estrangement, two siblings reunited through therapy and intentional conversation. They rebuilt trust over time, but occasional conflicts resurfaced. Instead of breaking apart again, they committed to monthly check-ins and agreed to pause and talk when emotions ran high. Their story reminds us that reconciliation requires ongoing effort, not a quick fix.

13.4 Societal Reconciliation Over Time

Societies that have faced division must revisit the past, learn from it, and continuously work toward a more inclusive future.

- Germany's ongoing reflection on the Holocaust includes education, memorials, and public accountability.
- South Africa's reconciliation work continues long after apartheid, with ongoing dialogue around inequality and justice.
- Truth and reconciliation efforts in Canada continue addressing the trauma of Indigenous residential schools.

These efforts show that national healing requires sustained will and openness to change.

13.5 Sustaining Reconciliation Through Support

Long-term reconciliation is nurtured when people feel supported:

- Community spaces for dialogue and reflection
- Access to mental health resources
- Encouragement from faith or cultural leaders
- Media that promotes unity and understanding

Healing multiplies when we do it together.

13.6 Personal Growth Through the Journey

Staying committed to reconciliation helps us:

- Become better communicators

- Deepen our empathy

- Strengthen our resilience

- Expand our capacity for love and forgiveness

Reconciliation changes the world, but it also transforms us.

13.7 Final Thoughts

The journey of reconciliation is ongoing. It's not always easy—but it is always worth it.

Every conversation you open, every grudge you release, every act of kindness you offer contributes to a more connected, compassionate world.

Let us continue this work—not just for ourselves, but for those who will come after us.

Because, after all: We are not enemies. We never were.

Conclusion

We Are Not Enemies After All

As we come to the end of this book, the journey does not end here. Reconciliation is not a destination—it's a way of living. It is a commitment to peace, empathy, and shared humanity in every interaction we have.

Reflecting on the Journey

Together, we have explored:

- The roots of conflict and how misunderstandings grow
- The power of listening and vulnerability
- The necessity of forgiveness and the courage to apologize
- The science behind our need for connection

- The tools for resolving professional and cultural disputes
- The danger of toxic group mentalities
- The long-term process of healing and reconciliation

Each chapter has offered insight, but more importantly, it has invited action.

We Are All Bridge Builders

You don't need a title or platform to be a peacemaker. Your influence begins in your home, your workplace, and your community. Each time you choose to listen, to forgive, or to extend kindness, you are building bridges where there were once walls.

You may never see the full impact of your efforts, but seeds planted in love and courage often grow in quiet, powerful ways.

A Call to Continue

Let this book be a beginning. Continue the conversations. Challenge division. Stand up to injustice. Be patient with yourself and others as you walk the path of reconciliation.

Remember:
- Peace begins with empathy.
- Healing begins with honesty.
- Reconciliation begins with you.

We are not enemies.

We are human.

We are connected.

And we are capable of something better.

Let us go forward—together.

Because after all… We are not enemies. We never were.

Final Call to Action

As you close this book, remember that reconciliation isn't a one-time gesture—it's a lifestyle. You don't need to be a public leader, a scholar, or an expert to make a difference.

You can start right where you are:

— Reach out to someone you've grown distant from.

— Start a conversation that you've been avoiding.

— Be the listener someone else needs.

— Create space for others to be seen, heard, and understood.

Speak with intention. Forgive with courage. Act with love.

Share what you've learned. Invite others into the process. Be the example of unity in a divided world.

And when you feel discouraged, come back to these words:

We are not enemies. We never were.

Now go—build bridges. The world needs you.

Final Thoughts

The journey of reconciliation is ongoing. It's not always easy—but it is always worth it.

Every conversation you open, every grudge you release, every act of kindness you offer contributes to a more connected, compassionate world.

Let us continue this work—not just for ourselves, but for those who will come after us.

Because, after all: We are not enemies. We never were.

Made in United States
Orlando, FL
27 June 2025